Poems Amidst the Piety

A poetic commentary on Christian culture

SAM LEES

With illustrations by Draw Near

Copyright © 2023 Sam Lees

All rights reserved.

ISBN: 9798388413352

For Becci. Always.

CONTENTS

	Introduction		
1	**Trench Warfare**	26	**Glory Spray**
2	Baptism Enquiry	27	Searching for Believers
3	**Transfigurating Churches**	28	**Six Strings and Skinny Jeans**
4	Are You Coming Back?	29	Imposter Syndrome
5	**The Epistle to the Church in England**	30	**Imago Dei?**
6	Take a Compliment(arian)	31	Christians Say the Cringiest Things
7	**The Good Student**	32	**A Question of Heaven**
8	Let Us Play	33	Hope for the Homeless?
9	**Questions?**	34	**A Creed to Fall By**
10	Robes of Hypocrisy	35	Limits of Acceptance
11	**Schemin' Demons**	36	**Church Coffee**
12	Beati2d's	37	One Body?
13	**Know Your Worth**	38	**Searching Symptoms**
14	Bipolar Believers	39	Hermeneutical Humility
15	**AD-JC**	40	**Eye See You**
16	Heelys on Hallowed Ground	41	Welcome
17	**Celestial Riots**	42	**United?**
18	Proper Preaching	43	God Boxes
19	**In Fact…**	44	**The Search for Grace**
20	Since You've Been Gone	45	Our Lovely Church
21	**I'm Not a Universalist, but…**	46	**The Lord's My Audiologist**
22	Holy Quartet	47	Easy Like a Sunday Morning…
23	**Big Questions**	48	**Limited Jesus**
24	Why wait?	49	Pilgrims Without Progress
25	**Cynically Synodical**	50	**Holey Holiness**

ACKNOWLEDGMENTS

I have to give a huge shout out to Draw Near, who have provided all of the illustrations in this book. I approached an artist known for vibrant colour and asked for black and white sketches, and still the outcome is amazing.

Check out the full collection of Draw Near art at:

DrawNear.co.uk

INTRODUCTION

About me:
I guess I should introduce myself. I am a thirty-something Christ-loving person. Ordained in the Church of England since 2022, serving at the time of writing in the same council estate I grew up on... or refused to do so. I wrote a couple of poems as a kid in school, but lifestyle and hunger for street-cred soon steered my creative writing into a lack-lustre rap career. Whilst trying to make music that glorified violence, drugs and petty theft; I was living the same. Thankfully I was introduced to Jesus by way of an irreconcilable encounter and managed to find a new path in life that directed me away from the violence, drugs, theft... and terrible music.

I was drawn back to music as a much-needed creative outlet, but with a new twist. I began making gospel-rap music (whatever that is) and had nominal success recording and performing Christ-centred hip-hop over a number of years, even picking up some awards along the way.

Then something strange happened... I realised I was getting a bit old for the rap image. My music to my kids was the equivalent of those memories you might have of your dad dancing at weddings. Cringe. I put the music to bed, and took a break whilst training for ordained ministry. After a few years of stubbornness, I gave in to the constant nagging of my loved ones to rekindle that creative side of me, I began to write some fun sentences and before I had paused to make a plan for something serious – I had written this poetry book.

I have spent time in all manner of traditions and denominations, and love and challenge them all in different ways – no churches were harmed in the making of this book!

About this book:
This collection of poems, ideas and limericks began as a Lenten discipline, trying to reignite my passion for creative writing. Having a Twitter account that follows Christians from varying traditions, denominations and

persuasions meant that I had no end of inspiration. Poems Amidst the Piety draws on the differing views of many of these, as well as my own observations, to create a commentary of Christian life and church politics that is both satirical and sadly accurate.

You may be expecting clever imagery and articulate writing.
You may be expecting the theological musings of an artistically eccentric poet-type.
You may be expecting something that fully grasps and accentuates the beauty of the English language…

If so, you may be disappointed.

The only way I can really sum up my style of poetry, is with a poem…in my style. So though this is not really one of the poems for this book - it is a poem, that is in this book.

Enjoy.

> I wish I could write poetry
> Like proper grown-ups do;
> The type that doesn't need to rhyme
> And sounds well clever too.
>
> I'm really not that cultured,
> I've no respect for prose…
> However smart your metaphor
> It still seems like a pose.
>
> The poems I appreciate
> Are the same ones that I write -
> So feed me lines of equal length
> …The Humpty-Dumpty type.
>
> Most other forms are dead to me
> And to be frank they bore me,
> A poem with no rhyming in
> Is just a rubbish story.

Shall we begin?

1. TRENCH WARFARE

As I witnessed the cheap shots being fired between Christians, I wondered if either extreme of conservative or progressive theology really followed Jesus in this battle, whose camp would He be in?

Upon the fields of Christendom
Are trenches right and left,
Technically they're all for one
But still fight to the death.
Some welcome in too many folks
The type the right rejects -
And rather than just disagree
They've made a right old mess.

They might call it a holy war
Claim they're protecting Christ,
They forgot to check the depth of it
And stepped out on the ice.
So, fights arose from little feuds
No hope was kept alive
Into the trench they jumped, to fight
For the pensions and the tithes.

Pastors pace the war room floor
Keeping warm within their nest
They fire bad theology
From the trenches where they rest.
No one treads the in between
That open ground ahead
But it's in that very no-man's-land
Jesus meets with the oppressed.

Poems Amidst the Piety

2. BAPTISM ENQUIRY

I have been in meetings with other clergy as well as in conversations with church members, where the fact that we baptise "non-churchgoers" is raised as a frustration… how high should we set the bar?

We only baptise locals here...
I've not seen you around
Have you got some proof to show me, dear?
Your address can't be found.

We only baptise regulars...
I've not seen you at church,
Nor your kids at Sunday School
I don't know which is worse.

We only baptise members now.
The type that tithe at least -
Our treasurer can set it out
You just need to sign the sheet.

We only baptise rota'd folks...
Do you read or make the tea?
I'm sure you can be shown the ropes
And commit to one in three.

We only baptise vicars' kids...
That way we guarantee
They'll turn up more than Christmases
And grasp theology.

We'll only baptise Jesus here...
He's the only one we want,
No one else is good enough
Let's cover up the font.

Poems Amidst the Piety

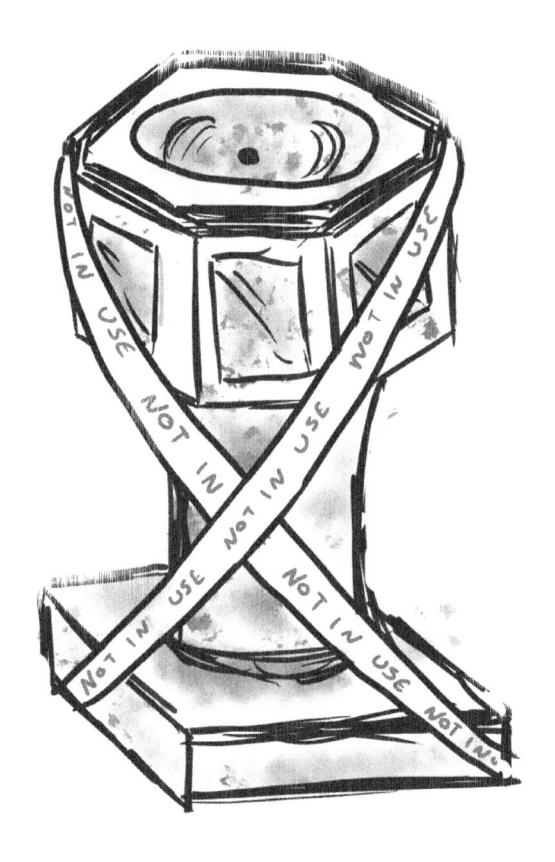

3. TRANSFIGURATING CHURCHES

We can get so caught up in politics and semantics that we lose focus on the real goal, to bear witness to the transformational power of God. When there are so many things that try to steal our focus, lets head to the mountain.

We're called to be a presence
Not a relic of the past
We trade regeneration
To be elevating scars
Colonialist tendencies
And patriarchal past -
Forgetting how few priests of old
Were saved upon the ark.

We claim that we repent
Yet still refuse to try reform
In love with age old empires
Just check the mitres worn -
By bishops as they guide us
In the midst of silent storms.
Pretending there's no locusts,
But we're fighting off a swarm.

We pretend it's our semantics
That define the God we serve
That grace we're freely given
We say they have got to earn
A price we put on everything
"You're paying not to burn!"
A toll booth on the narrow path
That really costs the earth.

I know there is a hope but still,
That hope is growing slim.
Those calling for a schism
Will make sure that no one wins.
Knowing every law, is shown
As more than knowing Him…
As for me, I'm climbing mountains
In the search for glowing skin.

4. ARE YOU COMING BACK?
Based on the real experience of a believer, who was so downtrodden by her church, but still going out of some strange sense of loyalty (or perhaps Stockholm syndrome) – yet when she left that place, she really found God.
Nobody should have to leave their church to find God.

Are you coming back to church? They say,
You're welcome if you do.
We'll give you back your favourite mug,
And empty out your pew.

Are you coming back to church, my dear?
We've noticed that you're gone...
Next week will be our summer fete,
We need your famous scones!

Are you coming back to church this week?
It's been a month or two.
By now you must be missing God,
He's waiting *here* for you.

Are you coming back to church at all?
Is it 'cos of what we said?
It's not that you're not treasured here...
... it's just pastors should be men.

Are you coming back to church or not?
We've not received your tithe.
We prayed for you at PCC.
Come back, and peace you'll find.

So, you've still not been to church, again,
You've clearly lost your way.
We checked with the authorities,
You've not been locked away.

If you do come back to church someday,
You'll have to start afresh.
I hope you find more faith by then;
The type that lasts, like marker pen.

Little did they know the truth -
She's not doubting, she's not lost.
She's not coming back to church,
It's since she left that she's found God.

5. THE EPISTLE TO THE CHURCH IN ENGLAND
What would St. Paul write to us, given the state of the Church today? What behaviours would he condemn in us? Would he even bother?

I was hoping to write this to praise ya'
But instead, I must address your failure
You're so far fallen in fact,
I'll start all this from scratch...
Let me introduce Jesus, your saviour.

Poems Amidst the Piety

6. TAKE A COMPLIMENT(ARIAN)

As surprising as it is for many outside the Church looking in, women are still treated as second to men in many churches. These are some of the scars in our patriarchal reading of scripture that need addressing and correcting, it certainly wasn't Jesus' way. (Start to the rhythm of a limerick)

"The Church, it is not patriarchal,
We don't give more power to men...
...But we don't allow bras in the pulpit,
Please read Timothy 2 once again"

Why does Paul always seem to trump Jesus?
Isn't Jesus the head of the Church?
The same Jesus who championed women
Again and again, He restored them their worth.

Men try really hard to devalue
The examples we see in the book
Lydia, Priscilla and Deborah
There's more if you care just to look.

It was Mary who told the disciples
That Jesus had slipped from the crypt,
Remove women from preaching
The Gospel to men...
And Christianity wouldn't exist.

Poems Amidst the Piety

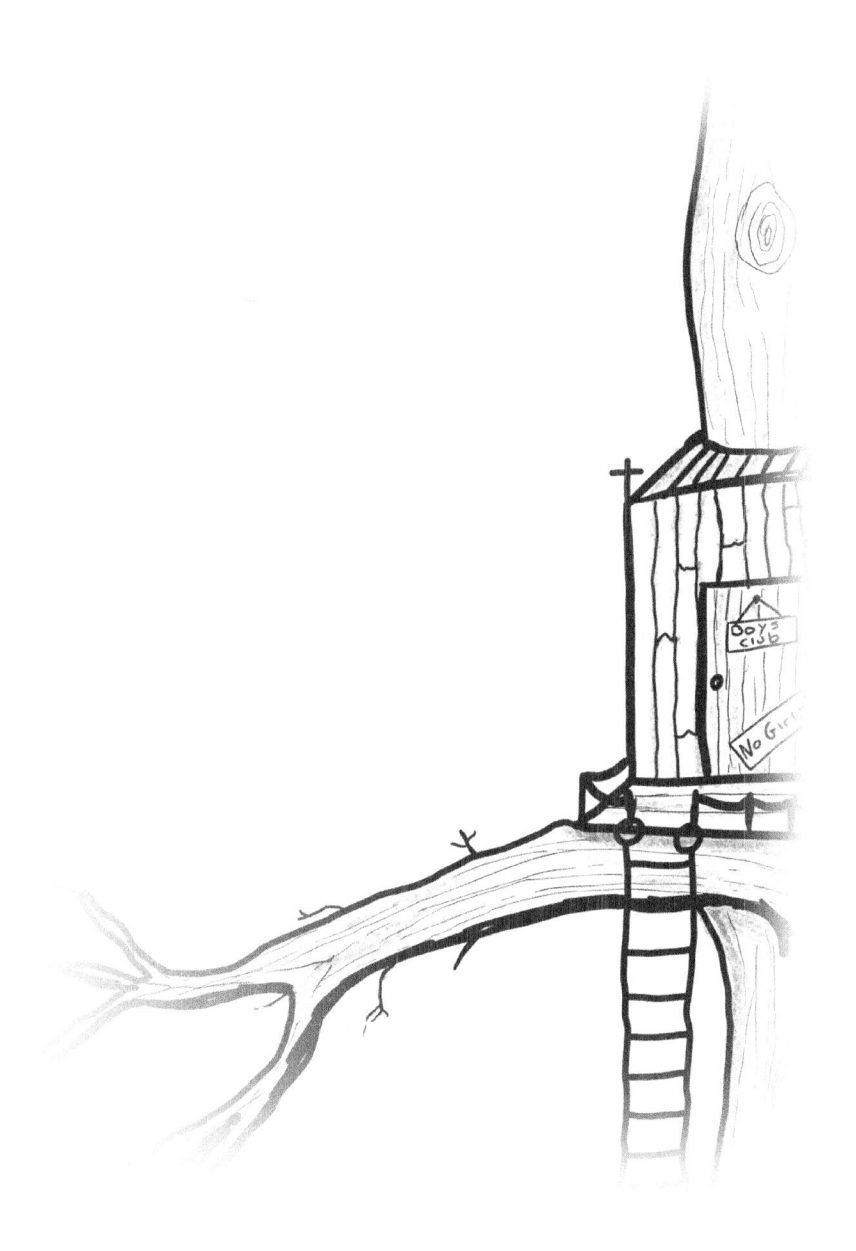

7. THE GOOD STUDENT
Jesus' teachings are controversial, some more than others. Jesus said to love and bless your enemies, and I'll be like "...really?"

I'm working through the teachings,
Of Jesus in the book.
I started at my neighbour's door
Returning what I'd took.
I read through the Beatitudes,
I re-learned how to pray,
Now I'm searching for my enemies
So I can roundhouse *bless* their face.

Poems Amidst the Piety

8. LET US PLAY
I can barely mention God on Twitter without some loving sibling-in-Christ calling me a heretic - it's great fun - but there are other, more family-friendly games you can play.

Do you want to play a game?
It's not Chess or Hide and Seek,
It's called "Colour Me a Heretic"
They play it every time I speak.
It's a bit like Snakes and Ladders,
As I'm climbing from their snares
To try proclaim the Gospel
Whilst they bludgeon me with theirs.
Do they really have a Cluedo,
About how to live in Christ?
And love others like he loves us,
At the Risk of living right.
Be careful with their invite
There's a Mouse Trap at the door,
They Scrabble for a hateful verse
that proves how they are pure.
It's like staring down a Battleship
That will swap your love for hate;
It's theological Jumanji
And I beg you not to play.

Poems Amidst the Piety

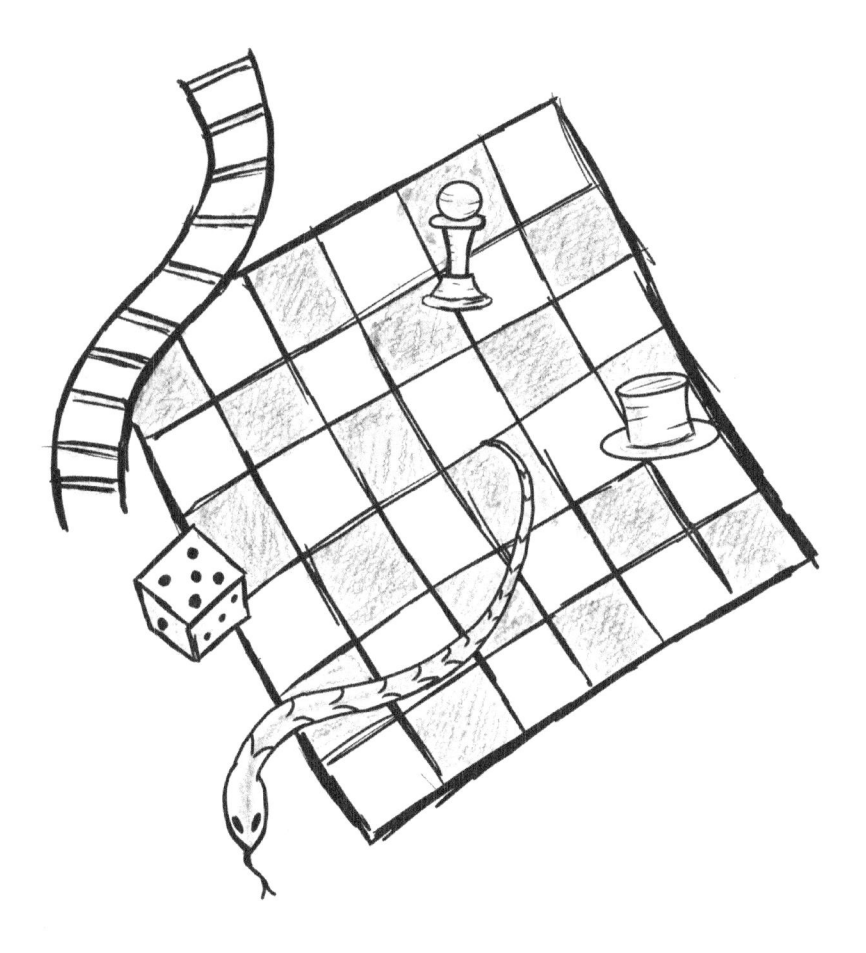

9. QUESTIONS
I see many churches that are very pleased to let their seats get filled by a diverse group of people, but refuse to answer straight-up questions. You are welcome, but your questions are not.

I feel called, is there space for preaching?
Leave your questions at the door.

Do you hold to ALL of Moses' teaching?
Leave your questions at the door.

How do you keep strong in temptation?
Leave your questions at the door.

Isn't there more than one translation?
Leave your questions at the door.

My sawdust? What about your log?
Leave your questions at the door.

Are you sayin' the Bible's one with God?
Leave your questions at the door.

Why is that man rolling on the floor?
Leave your questions at the door.

How much of tithes will help the poor?
Leave your questions at the door.

Is that youth pastor a little strange?
Leave your questions at the door.

And the preacher drives a custom Range?
Leave your questions at the door.

Could God be doing something new?
Leave your questions at the door.

God accepts me, but do YOU?
Leave your questions at the door.

10. ROBES OF HYPOCRISY
The shortest poem in this collection, quite possibly my favourite.

Priests on Christian Twitter
Are going quite berserk;
They're throwing hate at drag queens,
Yet **they** wear a dress to work.

Poems Amidst the Piety

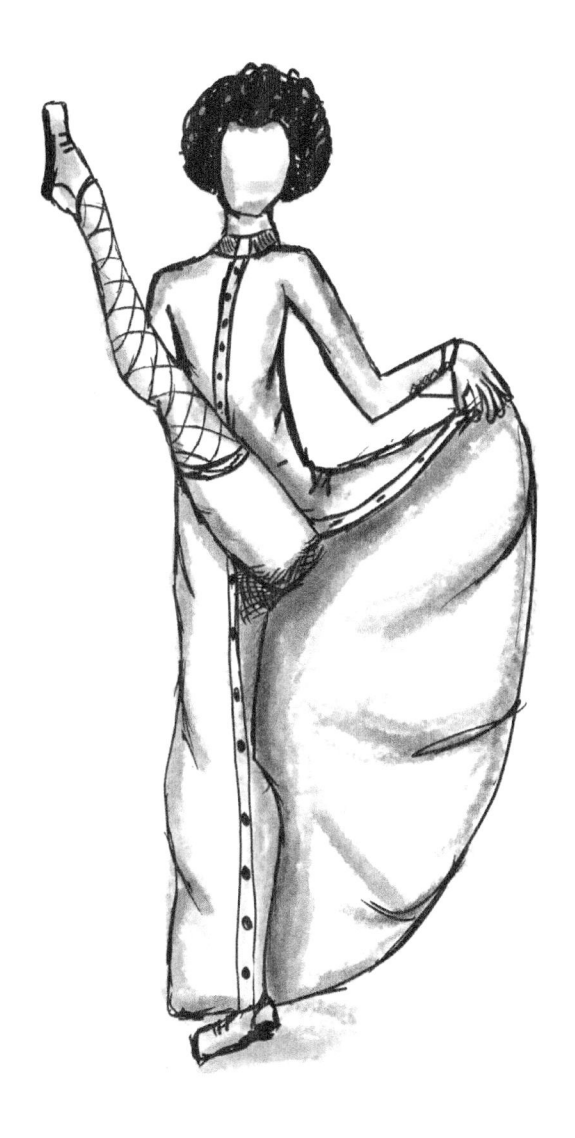

11. SCHEMIN' DEMONS

A bunch of Christians coming together for worship and fellowship is a lovely image, just imagine how encouraging and supportive they must all be to their church leaders… For some, it doesn't always feel that way!

I'm fighting with these demons
That want to see me fall,
Out of all my enemies
They are the worst of all.
They point out every error
They try to trip me up.
If I gave out birthday invites
They'd no doubt rip them up!
They attempt assassination
With suspect apple tarts,
Their feedback on my sermons, has
Become like poisoned darts.
These demons keep on coming,
Every Sunday's nothing new.
Can't you see them?
Look, they're everywhere -
They're filling every pew.

Poems Amidst the Piety

12. BEATI2D'S

One of the most controversial sermons of all time, still not understood by many today. Who is blessed?

Blessed are the affluent,
Blessed those who beg.
Blessed who support the blues
And blessed are the reds.
Blessed is suburbia,
Blessed are the blocks.
Blessed are the hip-hop fans
And blessed those who rock.
Bless'd are those with steadfast faith
Blessed are the shaky…
Blessed are the short in height
And blessed are the lanky.
Blessed are the managers
Blessed are the grunts.
I loathe to say this one out loud:
But blessed *is James Blunt*
Bless'd are those that dye their hair
Blessed are the bald,
Bless'd the wet behind the ears
And blessed are the old.
Blessed are the organised
Blessed are the ditzy,
Blessed are the dressers-down
And blessed are the glitzy.
Blessed are the patient
And blessed those who rush.
Bless'd is every one that hears
That Jesus died for us.

Sermon on the mount

Take: 2

Director:

Location:

13. KNOW YOUR WORTH

This limerick came from an argument between two people about how much money should be given to their church, the one who gave less ended up being shamed. I couldn't help but think of the parable of the widow's coins.

There was a young man in the service
Who showed no particular purpose
He was shooed out the door
As they knew he was poor
They forgot at which price he was purchased.

Poems Amidst the Piety

14. BIPOLAR BELIEVERS

"Love the sinner, hate the sin" — this statement is often used to justify hatred and mistreatment of entire groups of people, it is also a ridiculous front. You cannot love someone into changing, if that is the case you never truly loved them.

I really, really love you
Stop living in this sin!
You are so very welcome
Don't let the devil win!

I'm so glad you could join us
Your lifestyle is depraved!
I treasure our connection
Let's pray it all away!

You'll find us so inclusive
No prayers of blessing here!
You really can just be yourself
Don't let them know you're queer!

It's clear that Jesus loves you
You should live biblically!
The only way I'd love you more
Is if you were more like me.

Poems Amidst the Piety

15. ADJC

Being a church leader with ADHD is an interesting combination. Being fully present in worship whilst also wondering "is that feather from a pigeon or a seagull?" can be a task... Here is a brief insight.

A church might be the perfect place
To study the divine
But my mind is off on tangents
A large proportion of the time.
I really try to focus,
To follow as they read
While my brain is gripped by hunger,
That this reader will not feed.

What happened to the gold,
And frankincense they got?
Did they put them in the attic,
Did they sell them for a lot?

Has the Spirit ever dressed up
As a ghost for Halloween?
Were the dinosaurs created
Just to turn to gasoline?

What did that apple taste like
That Satan handed Eve?
Would Jesus be a cannibal
If he ate lamb at the feast?

Poems Amidst the Piety

What temperature is heaven?
Why does cake make us fat?
And that really burning question:
Why create the gnat?

All important questions,
That the Bible doesn't teach...
Then suddenly, all eyes on me...
Oh crap - I'm here to preach!

16. HEELYS ON HALLOWED GROUND

Have you ever been there, a child creaks the wooden pews and is instantly met with a "shhhhhh" that would put the strictest of librarians to shame? We have five kids, so have seen our fair share of interesting attitudes!

Can you not just keep it down?
This is the house of God.
I'd suggest you keep them still
And make sure the shouting stops.
It's hard enough to hear, you see
When you get to my age -
And their shuffling around the pews
Just made me lose my page.
It's great to see the young ones
It really makes my day,
But back when I was that size
Well, we knew how to behave.
So, do try to control them,
So they show us some respect
Church is for us grown-ups, so
Could you leave them home instead?

Poems Amidst the Piety

17. CELESTIAL RIOTS

Remember the Capitol riots? I remember seeing the news coverage and being like "what the actual...heavens". This got me thinking, would these same people try the same in Heaven if they stumbled upon Jacob's Ladder?

Can we storm the gates of Heaven,
Like they did the Capitol?
We can bundle past St. Peter
Dress code: casual.

Can we storm the gates of Heaven?
It wouldn't be a waste -
Although I'm sure I've got a spot,
I wouldn't mind a taste.

Can we storm the gates of Heaven,
Bring the pagans back some proof?
We can rub it in their faces;
See, we told you it's the truth.

Can we storm the gates of Heaven?
Put our feet up on the desk,
Scratch in some graffiti
Underneath the holy crest.

Can we storm the gates of Heaven?
It's our birth right after all.
I've got a thousand questions
That I need to ask St. Paul

Can we storm the gates of Heaven?
Not to weigh up what it's worth,
But to rise above our troubles
And leave depression back on Earth.

Poems Amidst the Piety

18. PROPER PREACHING

You know the sort. Those Christians that share images of hell's fire with "we warned you" written at the bottom... Or pictures of the Bible with swords and crusader's shields... Those that shout "COME TO GOD OR DIE!" Rather than "Come to Christ and live".

I want to hear a preacher preach
The way a preacher should.
With hell and fire and gnashing teeth
Let's scare them to be good.
I don't want the whole Bible read
Just a couple books will do:
Leviticus and Revelation,
They seem to ring true.
The middle bit's a bit too woke
All this "love" and "let them come".
Life should be pure sacrifice
Not joy, and hope, and fun.
I want to hear a preacher preach
The way they used to do,
When crusaders were idolised
And every church had pews.
I just want to live the glory days
When Jesus was still white
And other faiths would hide from us
And cower from our might.
I want to hear a preacher preach
And show me how to hurt ya'
Then I'll say I'm "Evangelical"
And get away with murder.

Poems Amidst the Piety

19. IN FACT…

I wonder what Jesus really thinks of how He planned for His Church to be, compared to what we have made of it. On paper it should be a foretaste of Heaven… in reality, well, you know…

Church should be a fairy-tale
Where everything goes right.
In fact: it's like when Roadrunner
And Coyote collide.

Church should be Utopia
A place that's lush and green.
In fact: it's more like Mad Max 2:
A world destroyed by greed.

Church should be a loving place
That nurtures all who come.
In fact: it's more like Cillit Bang
Just really tough on scum.

Church should be the hero
That's saving every soul.
In fact: it's more like Thanos
On a rampage for control.

Church should be legit
It should always stand upright.
In fact: the Church is Quasimodo
Hiding from the light.

Church should be so radiant
The bride that profits Him.
In fact: it's drunken bridesmaids,
Passed out and vomitin'.

Poems Amidst the Piety

20. SINCE YOU'VE BEEN GONE

Do you ever just scream "Jesus, come back NOW!" We are clearly not doing great in His stead, this is a prayer I wrote, expressing our need for an intervention.

Dear Lord,
I know you know it all
In the greatest kind of way,
But things have gone quite badly wrong
Since you went away.
There's been years of oppression
And wars fought in your name,
Corruption in your churches
And pastors caught in shame.
The world seems pretty fallen,
There's so much we need renewed.
And **that article** from TGC
...Did you see that too?
I hope you get to hear this
And then answer if you do,
Is this something you can help with?
And can you do it soon?
If you could just end famine,
As a token of your love,
Or send a cure for cancer
With the gift tag "from above"
I know you're probably busy,
And your workload's pretty rough.
But please would you come back now?

With love,

From all of us.

Poems Amidst the Piety

21. I'M NOT A UNIVERSALIST, BUT…

There is a pattern online of universalists (those who believe everyone will go to Heaven) being painted out as the worst heretics of our time… when I look at the abuse perpetrated by clergy, the hate spewed by some conservative Christians in the name of God, and the other ways we twist God to abuse others… I begin to think "Are universalists all that bad?"

I'm not a universalist,
But I kinda wish I was,
I could abandon most theology
And never say I'm soz.

If I were a universalist,
I could probably take up drink.
Dance naked round the vicarage,
Not caring what they think.

The thing with universalists,
Is perhaps they hope too much.
But if I'm to burn for anything…
Let it be for too much love.

Poems Amidst the Piety

22. HOLY QUARTET

The Bible is a historical record that documents God's interaction with varying people groups over the course of time. It contains examples, both good and bad, which can shape our lives. It holds within it the covenant promises made by God to love us, and our covenant to do the same. But some people's view of the Bible is… a little strange.

I see some people worshipping
They sound and look like Christians,
But things get unfamiliar
The longer that I listen.

They're praying to the Father -
That's nothing new to me,
It's the way that Jesus taught us
And that's my go-to, usually.

They're singing songs to Jesus,
I love to do the same
There's like; 10,000 reasons
We should glorify His name.

They're waiting on the Spirit,
To whisper them a word.
They really seem excited -
I wonder what they've heard.

But then their list continues,
And here's where it gets odd…
They elevate the Bible,
As if it's one with God.

They claim that it's inerrant.
That it translates perfectly.
They think it's God in paper form,
Like the Guru Granth Sahib.

It's at that point I retreated,
This doesn't match the creeds,
They've turned the Holy Trinity
To a four-way fallacy.

23. BIG QUESTIONS

Imagine as we come to the Kingdom, we are allowed to ask one question, one question only. What would you ask? Something profound? My years of theological training have probably done little to tame my unfiltered mind.

If I could ask Jesus one question,
On the day of my own resurrection
It would have to be grand,
And I'd probably land,
on
"How did Trump win an election?"

Poems Amidst the Piety

24. WHY WAIT?

Imagine the scenario: We meet our Maker at the end, and God reveals that maybe we didn't get it all right... heck, we've probably messed most of it up! That should be something we are prepared for, yet so many refuse to accept their own fallibility.

Would you still wanna worship Jesus
If He came back with dreaded hair?
If He told you that you'd got it wrong,
Straight or gay; He never cared!

What if Jesus told you
That **everyone** will rise?
That Heaven's gates are open wide
Thanks to His sacrifice.

What if it transpired,
That our doctrines got it wrong?
And He told us all to start from scratch,
And make a Church where **He** belongs.

Would you willingly accept this,
And admit where you went wrong?
If the answer's "yes - when He comes back"
Why not try it whilst He's gone?

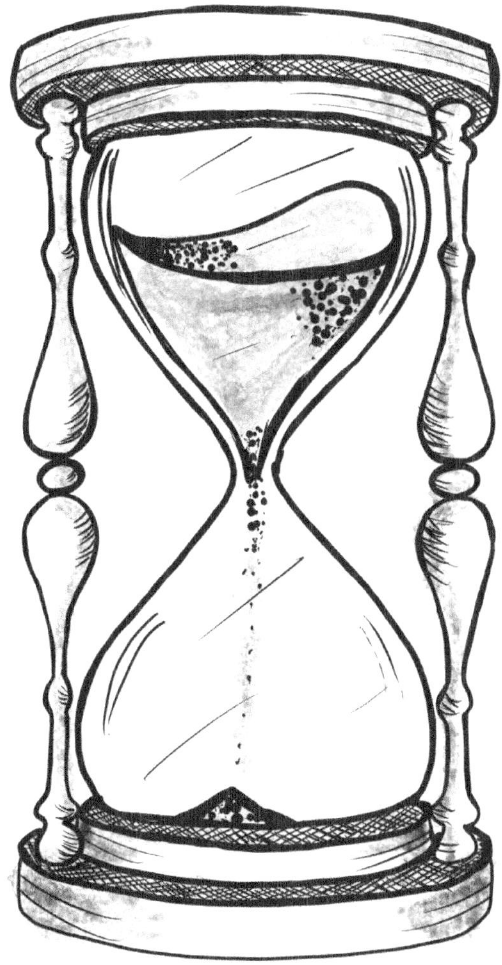

25. CYNICALLY SYNODICAL

The Church of England loves a synod, proper loves them. As well as sitting on local synods, I tend to watch the bigger ones online… but it is all a bit mad really. I actually wrote this during a deanery synod… Don't tell the Dean.

Let's put at each level a synod -
We can't call them councils or boards
But really, we know that they are,
And that every councillor's bored.
"But it's really a great little system"
I'm sure that's a feeling you've felt,
As the 17th member from Devon
Tries to amend, yet again, how it's spelt.
Let's put forward some needed direction
The proposer is setting the bar.
The amenders are not here to help,
But to prove just how clever they are.
It seems every 12-hour meeting
That is claimed to be needed by law,
Could really have just been an email
But instead, we've proceeded to war.
The smartest ones here will be snoozing
Knowing the business is done;
It's already been signed off in secret
Democracy's merely a front.
But for some, it is clearly important;
They give every motion its worth -
The reason the rest of us come…
Is to get several hours off work.

Poems Amidst the Piety

26. GLORY SPRAY

I had some fun with this one, thinking about what I would do if I had a Spirit-on-demand service on tap. What would you do?

I wish the Spirit was an aerosol
I could spray at an offence,
I could spray it at my neighbours
Over the garden fence,
I could spray it at my wallet
When I'm short a couple pence,
I could spray it at my lecturers
And help them make some sense.
I would spray it at the Bible
To gain universal truth,
Spray it at my wrinkled face
And reclaim back my youth,
I'd spray it at a war zone
And that day peace would win,
If the Spirit **was** an aerosol
No can could keep it in.

27. SEARCHING FOR BELIEVERS
Do you ever meet Christians in unlikely places? If we remove the standards and expectations created by a history of "purity culture" where might we find the truest Christians?

Did you know there's Christian pageants
Where they decide who's beauty-blessed
Christians in the fashion world
Who redefine our Sunday best.
Christians in the boxing league -
Fighting to provide.
Christians running OnlyFans,
And Christians that subscribe.
Christians in each industry,
All you have to do is search.
But sometimes still I wonder:
Are there Christians in the Church?

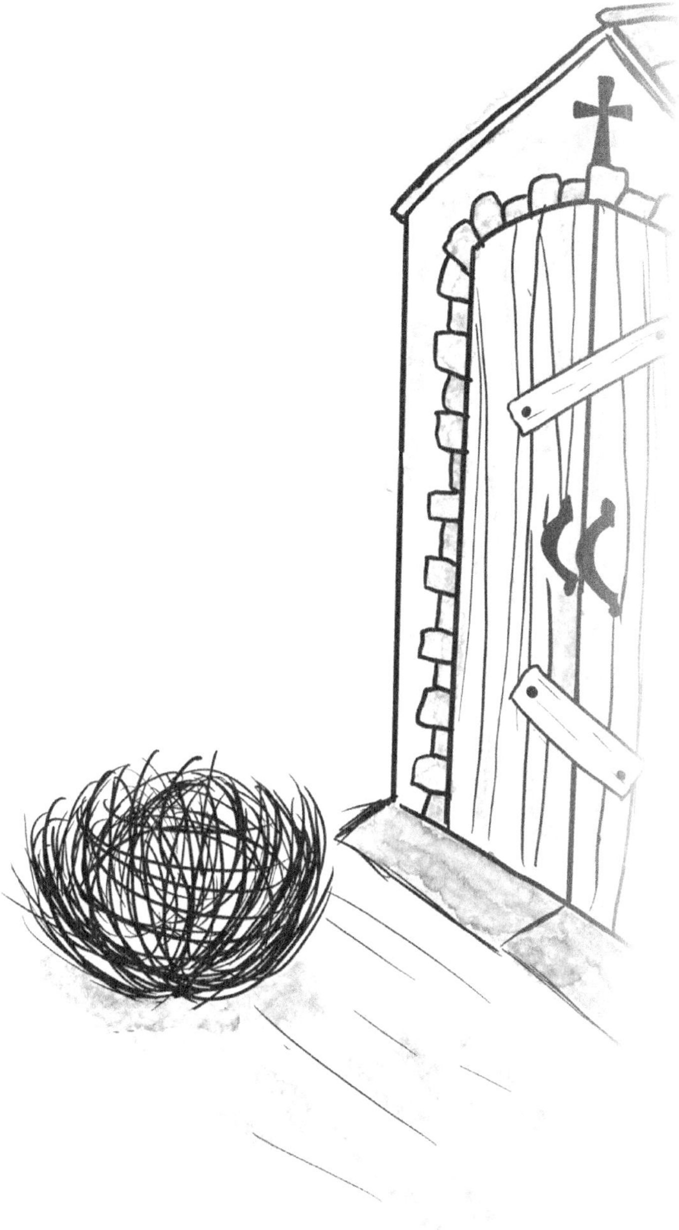

28. SIX STRINGS AND SKINNY JEANS

Some churches are a bit of a show, aren't they? It can be hard to see the worship through the smoke and lights... the really annoying thing is that they are always packed... regardless of their underlying theology. (I'm not bitter...)

Their church is like an island,
People coming from afar.
Seeking some euphoria
That comes from that guitar.

It's not about the liturgy -
In fact, that's pretty rare,
But if they have Nord keyboards
Then, the Spirit must be there.

Neon lights and sofas
Disguise old-fashioned thoughts,
Oh, to be a network church -
But still Anglican, of course.

Our parish church is not as big
Our youth group all but gone,
I visited this mega church
To see what we've got wrong.

All hands were raised in unison
One moment, that seems strange.
Is this prompted by the Spirit
Or by musical key change?

They focus on the band a lot
Is this Glastonbury or Church?
But their collection plate *doth overflow*
And maybe that's what hurts...

We need to pay our parish share,
As numbers still decline.
Could this be how we get them in,
From across the parish line?

See, I could wear a wristband
Saying 'what would Jesus do?'
If I had six strings and skinny jeans,
Maybe we'd be heaving too.

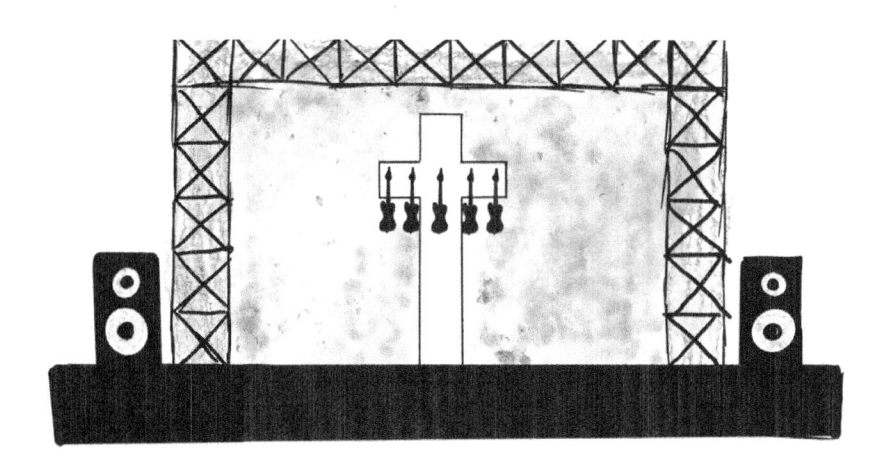

29. IMPOSTER SYNDROME

Coming from a rough background to ordained ministry is a bit of a rollercoaster, I often still ask God "are you sure?" ... to be honest coming from any background to ordained ministry is a weird move. This one is for anyone that feels they don't belong where God has called them.

This vicarage is massive
This collar's middle class
I feel like an imposter
But they tell me it'll pass.

My colleagues are well spoken,
That makes me the token chav
Need to swap out all my "innit though's"
For... "indeed's" - we'll go with that.

I'm tattooed and I'm common
And to be truthful not that smart,
Why God would call this person then,
I don't know where to start.

Most vicars seem so learned
So together and prepared,
As for me I'm kinda scatty
Disorganised and scared.

If this sounds familiar;
Relax, you're not alone,
And regardless of your background
God has called you; you are home.

Poems Amidst the Piety

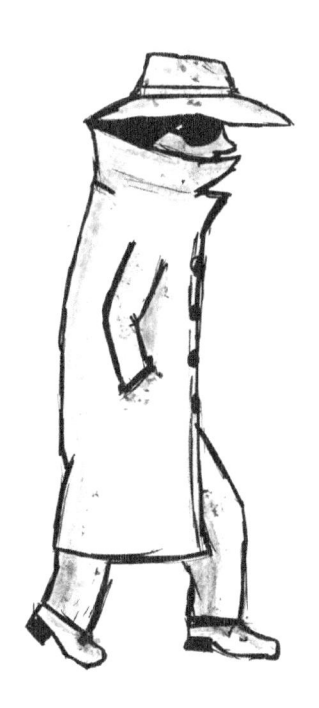

30. IMAGO DEI?

Some Christians on Twitter are vile. That is all.

"COVID was a hoax"
"The vaccine is a poison"
"Lefties go to hell,
And the queers are gonna join them"
"It's hard to be a man, that's
white and straight and middle class"
"The bishops are all heretics
Just sitting on their arse."
"Liberals are cancer"
"Jesus never smiles"
"Each refugee is evil"
and
"Drag queens are paedophiles"

The worst part of this hate
That it pains me to recite
Is that these are **actual** tweets
From people "representing Christ".

Poems Amidst the Piety

31. CHRISTIANS SAY THE CRINGIEST THINGS
Whilst on the subject of Christians on Twitter:

Have you ever scrolled through Twitter,
And mistakenly announced:
"They have *Christian* in their bio,
I wonder what they Tweet about..."

So, you delve a little deeper
to see them representing Christ,
But the nonsense that they're spouting
Makes you shrivel up inside!

They'll be asked by non-believers
"Why should I turn to God?"
"'CAUSE RIGHT NOW YOU'RE GONNA BURN IN HELL"
Is their rational response.

And they're the face of Christians
In this weird old Twitter-sphere
Picking fights for Twitter likes;
The keyboard ripper's here.

What a great example,
Of how weird believers are
But us normal ones stay silent,
And let these lot think they're stars.

Poems Amidst the Piety

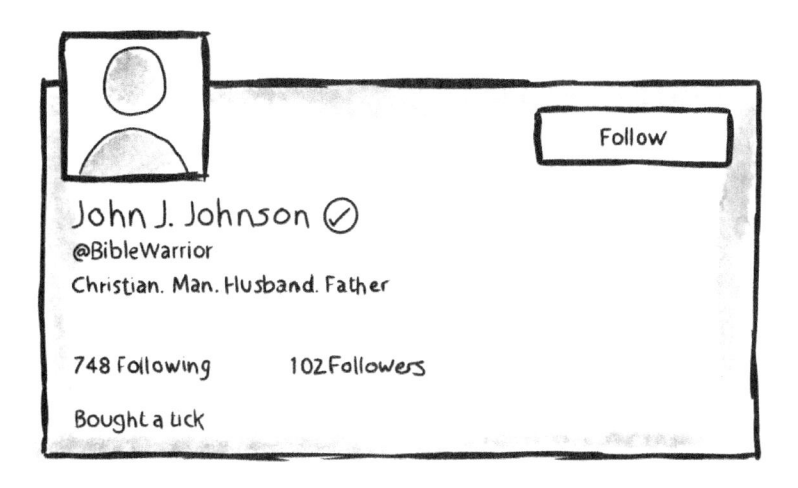

> John J. Johnson ✓
> @BibleWarrior
> Christian. Man. Husband. Father
>
> 748 Following   102 Followers
>
> Bought a tick

32. A QUESTION OF HEAVEN

What is God's Kingdom really like? How much have you thought about it? Is it a land of clouds and white tracksuits? Is it a motorway without traffic jams? What is on the dinner menu?? So. Many. Questions.

Is Heaven free from hunger,
Will the banquet ever end?
What's the status of fig-roll supply?
... I'm asking for a friend.
Can we mute the story telling folk
That drive us round the bend?
Can you cancel drunken messages,
Even after you've hit send?
Do the burning fires of hell
Heat the hot tubs of the righteous?
Is there week-long morning prayer
Just to satiate the pious?
Do they have a slim-fit option
At their clergy-shirt suppliers?
Is there calorie free ice cream
And a battered mars bar diet?
Will God show blooper reels, to help
Us laugh our fails away?
Is the postman always timely,
Bringing mail every day?
Is there a type of gaming, that
Doesn't buffer as you play?
And bathtubs you can lay in
If you're more than 4ft 8?

Does Heaven have a dress code,
Does it stretch to Jordan 4's?
Can you pause an online meeting
If you're unfortunately bored?
Do children have their freedom,
Or still forced to do some chores?

How do you picture Heaven?

Here's my questions,

How 'bout yours?

Godgle

🔍 | What is Heaven like?

Search

33. HOPE FOR THE HOMELESS?
It's one of the most basic Christian traits, isn't it? Feed the homeless. But how much more could we do if we scrapped the convenient excuse of "Our insurance doesn't cover that..."

"The Church really cares for the weak,
Like the Shepherd looks after the sheep"
**Their buildings are rent-free,
Heated, yet empty -
Whilst the vulnerable sleep on the street.**

Poems Amidst the Piety

34. A CREED TO FALL BY

As I look at common hateful comments from certain branches of Christianity, I ask myself: What must their creed look like? – Something like this I guess:

I believe in God the Father
I believe *my* church is ace
I believe that Christ would rather
I focus more on hell than grace.

I believe in God the Son
I believe we're doing great
I believe it will be fun
To watch you burn from Heaven's gate.

I believe in God the Spirit
I believe I know it all
I believe there is no limit
On how far down the woke will fall.

I believe in life eternal
I believe I might be dead
I believe this heaven's warmer
Than the one my pastor meant.

Poems Amidst the Piety

35. LIMITS OF ACCEPTANCE

Have you ever met a Christian that is so openly welcoming of all sorts of people, reaching out to rich and poor alike, meeting with other faith leaders to plan good deeds for the community… yet you let slip that you support the LGBTQI+ community and suddenly all hell breaks loose? All. Hell.

I could have tea with a Tibetan,
Share a supper with a Sikh,
See a movie with a Muslim
And not care what people think.
I'd spend a morning with a Mormon,
A spot of Jenga with a Jew,
Whatever your religion
I will make some time for you.
I'd play hopscotch with a Hindu,
Pass the parcel with 'em all…
**But I will not share my C of E,
With a flipping liberal.**

36. CHURCH COFFEE

I have had some of the best and worst coffee of my life in churches, with strong memories of those brown glass mugs… What does your coffee say about you?

Do you give a cup of comfort
When the service ends?
Or a cup of cheap and cheerful,
To limit monthly spends?
Are there many choices
Of cups to share with friends?
Or a cup of Heaven's banquet,
That most coveted of blends?
Are your cups half empty,
Or do they overflow?
Do your cups keep people in,
Or do you give them cups to go?
Do your cups come with a smile?
Do your cups come often cracked?
Do you serve a cup that's worthy,
For the day when He comes back?

37. ONE BODY?

We are all parts of one body, Jesus is the head, love is at the heart... so which part are these utter buffoons?

I think I have found a religion
That is hiding in obvious sight,
It smells something like Christianity
But is far from the teachings of Christ.

Jesus said love every neighbour
Don't block my children from me
They've twisted this simple commandment
To enforce their prescribed purity.

Jesus had come for the broken
His Gospel was brought for the poor
Yet the richest of folks in these churches
Use their wallets to hold closed the door.

They claim that the Bible is sovereign
That in English it's clear and concise
And that any perception that's different
Well, it's clearly a heretic's vice.

They cancel out years of tradition
No collars, and rush through the meal
Then claim that the gays are the problem
And they alone keep the C of E real.

Imagine if they had met Jesus
On the plains of the Near Middle East
I'm sure Jesus would call **them** the problem
And use their example to teach.

Poems Amidst the Piety

They cast doubt on everyone's faith
Kick them down, as a reason to gloat
They'd poke fun at the sinking St. Peter
As they laugh from the dry of the boat.

Let's be clear, this is not my religion
I really hope you can tell us apart
And if **they** are a part of the body;
They're an arse,
'Cos they can't be the heart.

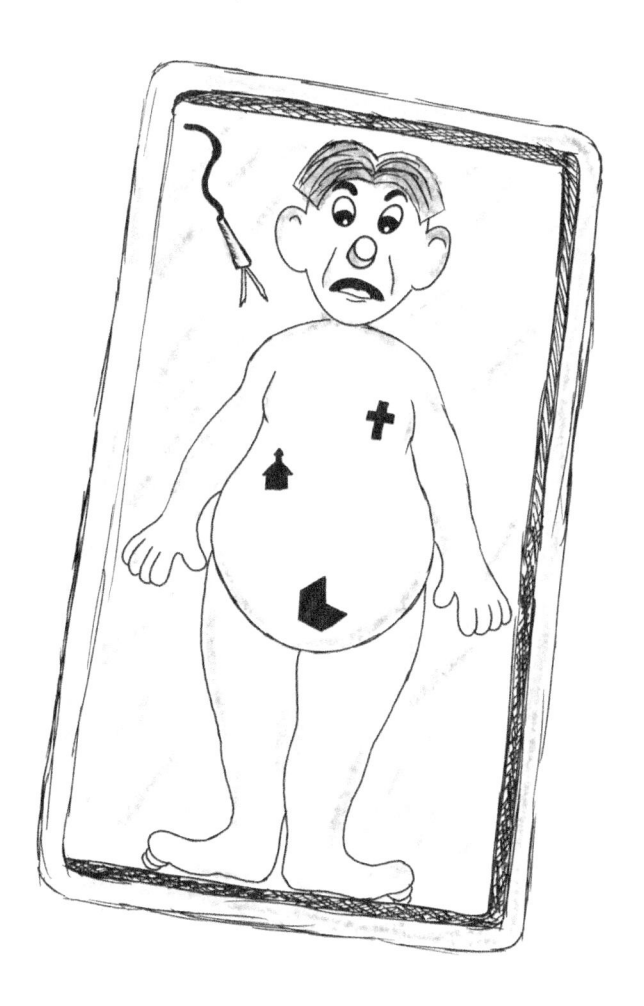

38. SEARCHING SYMPTOMS

When I found God, I was in a really dark place. I had no hope or direction until I opened myself to God. Many are struggling in these same dark places, without realising where the answer is.

Some search in the darkest of places
Some search in anxiety's grip
Some search in the bottles they empty
Or in the white lines that they sniff.

Some search in the smoke they inhale
Some search with a blade to their skin
Some search while subjecting their loved ones
To the same pain that they're feeling within.

Some search by abandoning friendships
Some search on those internet rooms
Some search buying all things designer
Like the debt might alleviate gloom.

Some search without anyone knowing
Some search in adrenaline highs
Some search with a new set of wheels
All the while ignoring the signs.

We search for that something that's missing
For something to switch our despair
Move that search up to Calvary's hilltop,
Every answer we need would be there.

39. HERMENEUTICAL HUMILITY

Living your life through the example you interpret from scripture is fine. But you need to be able to admit that there is a chance that you are wrong. The Bible is many things... but it is not always clear and concise! (The term Hermeneutical Humility was taken from a tweet by Dr. Kevin M Young – give him a follow.)

What was really parted,
The Red Sea or the Reeds?
Are we truly saved by grace
Or is there space for deeds?
What sin was it in Sodom;
Bad hospitality?
Or could it be a warning
For our sexuality?
When Moses left the mountain
Was he glowingly adorned,
Or were the artists right and he,
In fact, was growing horns?
Did Paul suggest that women
Should never speak, in any church...
Or was it just Ephesian ones
That would constantly converse?
Did Jesus speak of hell,
Or the local rubbish tip?
Could some of His hyperbole
Be wrongly seen as writ?

There is actually no way
We've got it all locked down
Though some do really think
That they deserve perfection's crown
In every single tongue,
Each translation that we see
Are pretty major differences
That form theology.

So, if somebody tells you
That they have it all correct
Know that when they meet their maker
That's a claim he'll soon reject.
We claim we're oh so smart
But still, **all** faith is based on trust.
So Hermeneutical Humility:
It really is a must.

40. EYE SEE YOU

So many hypocrites claim to be Christian. One thing the Bible is actually pretty clear on, is that this is not okay. Give grace.

They say:
I couldn't help but notice
A **speck** of sin there in your eye,
I'd thought I'd better point it out
As I was passing by.

Well, it's not so much a spec
It's kind of like - a **piece**...
I'm sure most people see it
Have you tried to blink, at least?

When I say a piece
I think I mean a **chunk**
Your sinfulness is blatant,
I knew somebody stunk.

Chunk might be too kind
In fact, a **lump** is more precise
I can teach you to be better,
Just heed to my advice.

That lump looks really bad
It's **gigantic**, it's a mess
It's the talk of the whole church
And it's causing us some stress.

She replies:
I've heard you loud and clear
And I'll take a look, of course
But first, I'll call a tree surgeon
To deal with what's in yours.

Poems Amidst the Piety

41. WELCOME
Did you know that most churches have a welcome team? A team of people whose sole job is to welcome people into the church… the question is: **What** *does your church welcome?*

We welcome the exclusion
Of women's ministry
We'll give you special bishops,
Some men that will agree.
And
We welcome the suggestion
Of the book's inerrancy
But not of mistranslation,
God spoke the KJV
And
We welcome invocations
Of hell, to those who sin.
And celebrity-like pastors
In the hope they'll bring them in.
But
We will not welcome couples
Whose genders are the same.
We will not welcome doubters,
Your questions bring you shame.
And
Whilst we welcome children
We welcome not their noise.
We do not welcome fidgeting
Nor do we welcome toys.
So
I think you'll see it's clear
Our doors are open wide,
And as long as you look just like us -
You're welcome here inside.

Prodigal church

~~All are welcome~~
~~Most are welcome~~
Some are welcome

Sunday @10

42. UNITED?

The only thing worse than a church leader with polarised views, is one that bites their tongue and sits on the fence to keep the seats filled. It is time to stand up, state your position, and deal with the consequences.

Christians are so varied,
On not much have we agreed.
In fact, we're always arguing
On all, *except the creed*.
The strongest on each topic
Will shout to all who hear;
Pretending they alone know God -
Rejoice, the prophet's here!

But some are hiding in the office,
Counting up the tithes.
Pretending that their loving arms
Like Heaven's gates, swing wide.
But harbour hidden viewpoints
That deserve some reprehense -
We're in need of some barbed wire,
To keep our leaders off the fence.

Poems Amidst the Piety

43. GOD BOXES

Our life experience, culture and theology all shape the box we put God in, none of us experience God in a vacuum, none of us are box-free.

What does your God box look like?
Do you keep it out on show?
Is it strapped with limitations,
Or do you give it room to grow?
Does your God box ever open,
To give God space to breathe?
Have you poked some air holes in, at least,
To offer some reprieve?
Has your God box been adapted?
And does it ever change?
Has it moved since you first made it?
Or has it stayed the same?
Is your God box proper sturdy?
Is it marked with fragile tape?
Would you let a stranger shake it,
Or do you worry it might break?
Do you covet other boxes,
That look good at a glance?
Did you know God would escape our boxes
If we just gave God a chance?

Poems Amidst the Piety

44. THE SEARCH FOR GRACE

This isn't as tidy as the rest, as it was written to be spoken/performed rather than read. Grace is mentioned 170 times in the Bible, yet lately I have been seeing very little of it between Christians with differing views on certain subjects, this is a rallying cry for believers to do better.

It seems that grace is what we're lacking in
Freely we were given yet secretly we're stashing it
...see the damage is -
We put God in a box and it ain't Jesus on the packaging!

Yet it's of Him that we've been fed
And He tells us to love more and sin less
Disagree without dis-tress
'Cause you know you ain't giving out grace with your fist clenched.

We say that love is what defines us,
We claim we're ready to bear fruit like a vine does
[Ha!] More like raisins man - we dried up
Focussed on divisions, not the Risen that unites us.

Take a minute with your eyes closed,
Imagine grace, that shining face up in those white robes
And that grace tells us to ignite hope.
And us? We turn a narrow path into a tight rope.

So Church, can we give each other love?
Can we offer out a hand instead of trip each other up?
If we're distracted by semantics then our mission's pretty stuffed,
And that's a pretty blatant failure when we're sitting with our Judge!

Breathe.

We're on a path we should take slow
Travel well together, and remember that our pay load;
Is in the wounds of the cross, from where grace flows...
So, love God, love people.
Case closed.

Poems Amidst the Piety

45. OUR LOVELY CHURCH

Church is people, not buildings. Church is people, not buildings. Church is people, not buildings.
Have you ever met people in church buildings that would rather study the walls than speak to the people? I have, including church leaders. (It's pronounced love-er-ly!)

Our church is really lovely
10th century, I'd guess
The porch way is original
And older than the rest

Our church is really lovely
The tower is the crown
The spire is 300 feet
The tallest in the town

Our church is really lovely
With pews of solid pine
Tiles cracked, but period
They've stood the test of time

Our church is really lovely
The organ's just been tuned
We're not stuck in the past, oh no,
New hymn books coming soon

Our church is really lovely
The silverware is bright
Our cleaner's working overtime
No cobwebs left in sight.

Our church is really lov-
A question? yes please do.
The people? I don't see them much
But I'm sure they love it too.

Poems Amidst the Piety

46. THE LORD'S MY AUDIOLOGIST

Recently Martin Wroe challenged a meeting of clergy to reimagine Psalm 23, replacing 'shepherd' with another job. Having been recently diagnosed with notable hearing loss, this was the first thing that came to me. What are your ears blocked up with?

The Lord's my audiologist
He knows to say things clear,
Theology has blocked me up
And filters what I hear.

He claims I'm deaf to frequencies
That many people speak -
Subconsciously I block it out
If it's not what Luther thinks.

I wonder if it's all that bad,
The peace and quiet's lush
But He tells me it's selective,
And I'm missing out on much.

See, I filter universalists
And those obsessed with hell
- But in not hearing everyone
I've muted Him as well.

47. EASY LIKE A SUNDAY MORNING...

Wake up, get dressed, walk through those wooden doors, worship.
It can be so easy to take this routine for granted, for some people, engaging in worship as part of an institution that has marginalised, abused and tried to 'convert' them throughout its history – it is far from this simple. Be mindful.

Can you imagine the feeling?
Uncomfortably sat in a pew
It's not just the uncushioned seating,
But that everyone's staring at you.

It's probably just an excitement
That somebody new has arrived,
But what if it's really a judgement -
What if they saw you at Pride?

The anxiety seems to be winning,
You're planning your route to the door
Then suddenly music is playing -
No chance of escape anymore.

Maybe this church will be different
Maybe it's here that you'll thrive…
At least, they seemed really open
As you joined in their worship online.

Every whisper and grumble is torment
There's a chance that they're aiming at you -
Just like the first church that you went to;
Where the doctrine was hate and abuse.

If this all sounds like a long way,
From you comfortably going to church,
Then please do acknowledge you're lucky -
Because for many it's drastically worse.

Poems Amidst the Piety

48. LIMITED JESUS

Here's what I don't get. The same people who believe the miracles of Jesus, also put the biggest limits on Him… How can people believe that God created the vastness of our universe, governed by flawless mathematics, created the weirdest little insects and sea animals… Created the blobfish for goodness' sake! – yet somehow didn't create mankind with any sort of diversity?

You believe that He raised Lazarus
Back from an early grave,
Yet deny he'd go as far as to
Accept folk who are gay.
You believe that He Himself was raised
With nail scars in His hands,
But no way would He embrace
With anybody who is trans.
You believe that He was born
To a young virgin in the East,
But deny that He would ever call
A woman to be priest.
You believe that He restored the sight
Of many who were blind,
But deny that in His love
He could be moving with the times.
You seem to think He's limitless
Miraculous and true,
But somehow strangely impotent
When something threatens you.

Healing the Sick, Raising the Dead, Walking on Water & Hating the Queer

For Dummies

49. PILGRIMS WITHOUT PROGRESS

Christianity is better now than it has been in the past… Maybe in some ways, but some old habits die hard, and Christians just hide different hatred behind claims of "biblical loyalty".

It's clear that Christianity
Does have a chequered past,
Think back to the crusaders
Claiming Christ was in their hearts.
The building of those empires
Where lands were ripped apart,
The bishops that all voted
To keep slaves up in their yard.

The years in which the Church
Was making profit off of God
The poorest went to Mass
And come collection, they were robbed.
The clergy weighed up gold
That paid for them to live like slobs,
They claimed to be like Christ
But now, it is clear to see they're not.

Every Christian will admit that
In the past we earned our shame
"That was then, we're moving on"
Is something most of them might claim.
But the proof of the abuse
That still persists *in Jesus' name,*
Shows despite the constant fight
There's not a lot that's really changed.

Poems Amidst the Piety

50. HOLEY HOLINESS

Most of those that spend their time criticising the lifestyles of other Christians, are far from the 'holier than thou' image they present. There's imperfections in their purity, and holes within their holiness.

They claim to love their wives
Yet turn their browser history off
Then brag about a time
That they said *no* to someone hot.

They wear a flannel shirt
With some Louboutins on the stage
Then use their Sunday preach
Just to promote their Insta page.

They want some adoration
For the person they've become
Whilst shouting in our faces that;
"THE DEVIL'S CLEARLY WON!"

And if you show the origins
Of why you disagree
They'll holler even louder;
"YOUR WHOLE LIFE IS HERESY!"

They do all of this in public,
Calling everybody *woke*,
Not seeing how ridiculous
They seem to normal folk.

Poems Amidst the Piety

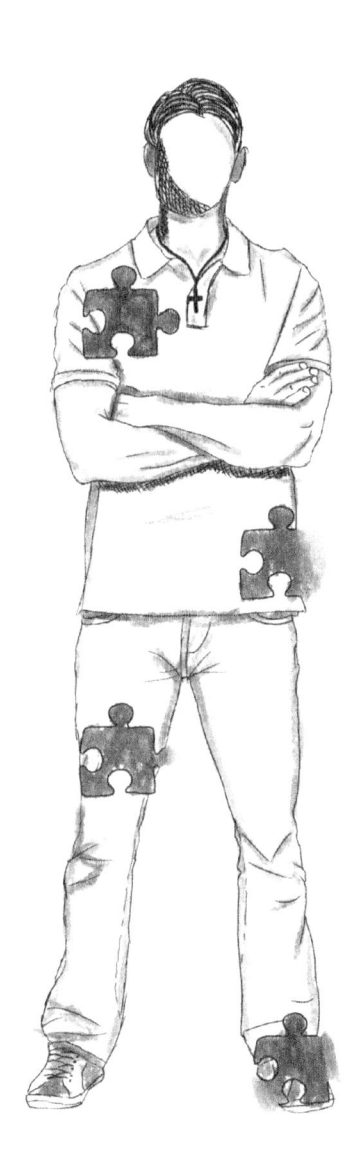

Printed in Great Britain
by Amazon